CW00853438

Cribl Stream Fundamentals

James L. Curtis

2

Preface

What this book is intended to be used for: This book is a primer on Cribl's features and capabilities. It will provide a general overview of Data Routing, pipelines, functions and more. It aims to communicate popular uses for Cribl Stream, explain features the product contains, highlight known best practices for using the product whenever possible. It also aims to help prepare you to take the Cribl Certified Observability Engineer (CCOE-SU) Exam.

What this book is not meant to be: An exhaustive list of everything that can be accomplished with Cribl Stream, or a comprehensive guide for all Cribl Stream deployments. There are many ways in which Cribl may be set up and to cover each scenario would be beyond the scope of an introductory book. An effort will be made to describe as fully as possible various approaches to setting up, configuring, and using Cribl Stream.

The Author (James Curtis) has spent his IT career in a variety of roles but has a passion for Automation, Big Data and Data Analytics. He wrote this book to help others who are early in their journey exploring Cribl Stream and who might not yet have discovered the tremendous value the product can provide or who understand the value but are looking for effective ways to communicate that value to Corporate Leadership.

Dedication

This book is dedicated to my Wife and two Daughters.

To my Wife Kaylynn, I want to express my deepest gratitude for the unwavering support you've given me. Your love and dedication are the cornerstones of my strength and success.

To Kallie and Kassie, our wonderful children, your presence fills my life with joy and purpose. The love and understanding of our family make every challenge worthwhile and every success more meaningful. Thank you for being my constant source of inspiration and for making our life's journey so beautiful.

Chapter 2

Deployment Types

There are multiple different ways you can deploy Cribl Stream. Cribl Stream can be deployed as a single instance or distributed as a part of a cluster of machines with a Leader and Worker nodes. You can do a traditional install on Linux hardware, you can deploy in a container, you can choose to utilize Kubernetes to scale dynamically, or you may opt to go with Cribl Stream's Cloud offering. You also can deploy into your own cloud infrastructure and you can also do a hybrid deployment, with a leader in the cloud and worker nodes on-premises. Which you decide to

17

use will depend largely on your requirements.

> **Exam Note:**
>
> When taking the CCOE-SU exam know that there are several Deployment Types. Single Instance, Distributed, Cloud, and Hybrid

2.1   Single Instance Deployments

A single instance deployment is great if you have a smaller amount of data, or do not currently have a need for redundancy. These deployments are great for those with smaller volumes of data and a single machine that can be easily recovered.

2.2   Distributed Deployment

A distributed deployment may be desirable for larger volumes of data or when redundancy is needed in worker nodes to ensure that data never gets missed. A distributed deployment involves deploying Cribl Stream to multiple computers, configuring one to be a Leader

Node and one or more machines to be worker nodes. Up to 1,000 Worker nodes are currently supported.

2.3 Stream Cloud

Cribl currently has a Cloud offering. They'll manage the hard stuff, installing Cribl, maintaining the infrastructure and you just worry about getting the data in and doing anything you see fit to it. What's not to love?

2.4 Hybrid Deployment

In some cases, having data leave your network unredacted, or without other alterations to the data may not be an acceptable solution. In cases like this placing a Cribl Leader in the cloud and using On-Premises worker nodes is a great solution to allow you to utilize the cloud service Cribl offers while maintaining more control about what gets sent over the internet and how.

2.5   Self-Hosted Cloud

It is easy to Deploy Cribl Stream into your own AWS Cloud using the pre-built Partner solution.

The deployment process on AWS involves the following key steps:

- Sign in to AWS Account

- Subscribe to Cribl Stream on AWS Marketplace

- Launch the Partner Solution

Before creating the stack, you must select the AWS Region from the top toolbar. You have options to deploy into a new VPC or into an existing VPC, with further choices between ARM64 and x86 architectures, and with or without VPC Flow Logs enabled.

2.6   Docker

Cribl Stream is easy to deploy using Cribl's Docker Container that can be found on Docker Hub. For more on Docker look later in the book on our chapter dedicated to deploying via Docker. Docker can be utilized in Single Instance, Distributed, and Hybrid Deployments.

2.7 Kubernetes

A Kubernetes deployment is beyond the scope of this book but know that helm charts for orchestrated deployments using Kubernetes do exist and are available in Cribl's Documentation.

Chapter 3

Installing Stream

3.1 Downloading & Installing

Regardless of which Deployment Type you choose installing Stream will start with downloading Stream at: https://www.cribl.io/download once downloaded you will un-tar the downloaded tarball to a directory of your choosing /opt/ is a good choice and we will assume that is the directory for the remainder of this book. An example of a command to download and install the latest version of Cribl can be seen below.

Make sure you are currently in the directory that you want to untar Cribl Stream in before running the below command.

<u>Downloading and Installing Command</u>

```
1  curl −Lso −  $(curl https://cdn.cribl.
      io/dl/latest−x64)  |  tar  zxvf
```

3.2 Starting & Starting on boot

After downloading and installing Cribl into your chosen directory you will need to start it and ensure that it starts on boot. You can do that with the following 3 commands.

<u>Enable Cribl boot-start</u>

```
1  cd $CRIBL_HOME/bin
2  ./cribl start
3  sudo $CRIBL_HOME/bin/cribl boot−start
      enable
```

These commands utilize the $CRIBL_HOME variable which is your installation directory by default. If the above command fails, try replacing $CRIBL_HOME with your installation directory. To verify that Cribl is installed and running you can run the following command.

Checking Cribl Status

```
1  cd $CRIBL_HOME/bin
2  ./cribl status
```

Chapter 4

Sources

In Cribl Stream a "Source" is what you use to define where your data is coming from. There are many types of sources. However, sources will either be, Push-Based Sources, Pull-Based sources, or Collector Sources.

4.1   Push-Based Sources

Push-based sources are sources of data that you can subscribe to that you can then receive. The initial source of that data determines what, how much, and how fast to send data. The data is pushed from the originating source and on the receiving end Cribl Stream listens for that data and accepts it in whatever form it is received. Samples of Push based sources include HTTP, TCP, Syslog, Splunk HEC and more.

4.2   Pull-Based Sources

Pull based sources are sources where Cribl will make a request to a source and that sources will then serve that data back. Examples of pull based sources include Amazon S3, Office 365, Splunk search and any other source where you might send a request to receive data.

4.3   Collector Sources

Collector Types

- Filesystem/NFS: This collector type is used for aggregating data from file systems or network file systems (NFS). It is particularly useful for accessing logs or data files stored on local or networked drives.

- S3: The S3 collector is designed for integration with Amazon S3 storage. It enables the extraction and processing of data stored in S3 buckets, making it ideal for cloud-based data architectures.

- Script: This type of collector allows the execution of custom scripts to gather data. It offers flexibility for collecting data from various sources or in unique formats that aren't natively supported by other collector types.

- REST: The REST collector is utilized for accessing data available through RESTful APIs. This is especially relevant for modern web services and applications that expose their data via HTTP endpoints.

4.3.1 Settings

On-Demand or Scheduled: You can configure the collector to run either on-demand or on a pre-defined schedule. On-demand execution is triggered manually, while scheduled runs are automated based on specified intervals.

Filter Expression: This setting allows you to define criteria to filter the data collected. Filter expressions can be used to include or exclude specific data elements based on your requirements.

Run Mode:

Preview: In this mode, the collector runs in a testing phase, allowing you to preview the data that would be collected without actually performing the collection process. Discovery: This mode is used to identify the types and formats of data available from the source, helping in configuring the collector more effectively. Full Run: In this mode, the collector performs its complete function, gathering and processing data as per the defined settings.

Exam Note:

When taking the CCOE-SU exam know that there are many different Sources. However, Sources generally come in one of 3 types Push-Based, Pull-Based, and Collector.

Chapter 5

Destinations

Destinations, simply put, are locations where you want to send your data to. Destinations come in multiple types, Streaming, Non-Streaming, and Output Routers.

5.1 Steaming Destinations

Streaming Destinations accept data in real-time or in small batches. The data is "streamed" from the source, through the pipeline and out to the destination in real-time or near real-time. Some examples or Streaming

Destinations include Splunk, Syslog, Kafka, statsd and more.

5.2   Non-Steaming Destinations

Non-Streaming Destinations accept data in batches or in set intervals. The data is accepted from the source, goes through pipelines, and is sent out in batches to the destination when certain configurable conditions are met. Examples of Non-Streaming destinations include S3 Storage, MinIO, and Local Filesystem storage. These destinations are great for short-term or long-term storage.

5.3   Output Routers

Output Routers are special meta-destinations that allow for rule-based selection of Destinations. For example, you may wish to send any data that contains PII or PHI to one destination and anything not containing that sensitive data can go to its own destination.

5.4 Other Destinations

There are a couple other special destinations to note. DevNull is a pre-configured output that just drops events. Linux Administrators may be very useful with the concept of DevNull. This Destination is useful for testing when you don't yet want data to start streaming to your other destinations. Default is as it sounds, if you have a destination where most of your data is sent you can configure it as the Default Destination. The Pre-Configured default is DevNull.

5.5 Backpressure

Backpressure is what happens when a destination is unable to receive data from Cribl Stream. There are a variety of reasons a Destination might experience backpressure. Most issues with backpressure usually are a result of either your Cribl Instance or your Destination not being sized appropriately for the amount of data being sent. When troubleshooting backpressure, you should begin by looking at the destination, working your way back to the source.

> **Exam Note:**
>
> When taking the CCOE-SU exam know that there are many different Destinations. Destinations are either Streaming, Non-Streaming, or Output Routers. In addition, there are two special Destinations. DevNull which drops events and Default which represents the Default Destination for Stream.

Chapter 6

Routes

Routes define the path the data will take as it goes through Cribl Stream. Quick Connect is an alternative to traditional Routes.

6.1 Quick Connect

Quick Connect provides a graphical representation to connect a Source to a Destination using a simple drag and drop design. Using Quick Connect, data goes directly from a source to its destination without the additional configuration needed for traditional Routes. Quick Connect is suitable for simple use cases where the need is simply to connect from a Source to a Destination with no added need for Filter Expressions using a Route. Using Quick Connect you can still utilize Pipelines and Packs to transform and shape your data.

6.2 Routes

Routes provide additional options to define the Path that data will take before it reaches Pipelines and Packs. This provides the ability to filter the data before it reaches a Pipeline or Pack as well as send the data through Pre-Processing Pipelines. Each route can only be associated with a single Pipeline and a Single Destination however it can have multiple associated Sources. It's important to note that the Destination that a Route is associated with can be an Output Router which uses Rule Based routing. Routes contain a filter expression. Filters are written in Javascript and evaluated as Boolean (true/false) values. Routes have the Final flag set to "yes" by default. Routes are evaluated in order from the top down. The main route should always remain at the bottom of the list and should serve as a catch all for any events that did not go down the above routes. It is important to note, any data that matches a route filter in a route with a final flag set to "yes" will never make it any further down the routes than they one it matches with. That is to say that when an event matches a filter, and the final flag is set to "yes" the event is consumed by the Route. When an event matches a filter, and the final flag is set to "no" then a clone of the event will be made and processed by the Route. The original event will continue to pass down the remaining routes and be processed by any routes that it matches with.

6.3 Route Groups

Route Groups are a collection of Routes that can be moved up and down the list of routes in unison. This is organization feature of the UI that makes is easier to organize and change the location of Routes that are dependent on each other if necessary. Routes still flow down the order they are in as described above.

6.4 When to use Routes vs. Quick Connect

You should use Routes when the ability to fine tune what data is needed to be sent to a destination. For example, when multiple data sets are coming in from a single source, or when you want to pre-process the data before sending it down a Pipeline.

You should use Quick Connect when a use case calls for simply sending data from Point A to Point B without a need to selectively route or process the data differently based on the content of the data coming from the Source.

Chapter 7

Pipelines and Functions

7.1 Functions

A function contains a set of Javascript instructions on how Cribl Stream should process data and tells Cribl Stream how to interact with the data passing down a Pipeline. There are many different types of functions that can drop, transform, mask, encrypt and further shape your data. Functions also contain their own set of Filters much like filters found in Routes. Only events that match the filters defined by the function are processed by that function. Functions can be moved up and down in the Pipeline to affect in which order functions get evaluated. Functions also contains a "Final" Flag. If Final is set to "Yes" then events matching the filter for that function are not sent further down the pipeline for processing.

7.2   Comment Functions

Comment Functions are functions that do not affect the data being processed at all. They simply allow you to place a comment above a function so that you can explain to others who might view a function you have written what that function does.

7.3   Normal Pipelines

A Pipeline is a series of functions organized in a list. Pipelines are where the actual processing of events happens. Events are sent from a route into a function. As with Routes, functions within a Pipeline are also evaluated in a top-down order. Stream contains 3 types of Pipelines.

7.4 Pre-Processing Pipelines

A pre-processing pipeline is a series of functions that allows you to act on your data before being sent down a route and their corresponding pipelines. This can be useful to condition data before processing for things like Timestamp extractions, or redaction of data before processing to ensure that later processing is more efficient.

7.5 Post-Processing Pipelines

A post-processing pipeline is a series of functions that allow you to act on your data after they have been routed but before they hit their destination. Reasons you might use a post-processing pipeline include masking or redacting data that you need for a route to ensure the data reaches the destination, but you might not want included in the destination itself.

Chapter 8

Cribl Packs

8.1 What are Cribl Packs?

Cribl Packs are pre-written modular blocks of code for specific use cases or Data Sets that can be exported and imported into Cribl Stream for re-use in another environment. Cribl Packs are a great way to re-use code among different Stream Environments or Worker Groups as well back up and save your existing Routes, Pipelines, and other Knowledge Objects.

8.2 Using Cribl Packs

You can think of Cribl Packs as a pre-packed tool bag. Filled with all the tools you will need to get the job done for a specific dataset or group of datasets. Need to Reduce Palo Alto traffic? Find the Palo Alto Cribl Pack and start your journey down an easier more stress-free data management for those data sources. To Import or a Create a New Cribl Pack go to Processing -> Packs and click the "Add New" button

8.3 Authoring Cribl Packs

Cribl Packs can be authored by community members and shared as well. Cribl maintains Pack Standards for how Packs should be authored here: https://docs.cribl.io/shared/packs-standards

8.4 Cribl Packs Dispensary

The Cribl Packs dispensary is a centralized location that all Cribl Packs can be pulled from. It is located here: https://packs.cribl.io/. The Packs Dispensary can also be used directly from the Cribl UI to add new packs.

Chapter 10

Filters & Expressions

10.1   Filter Language

All filters and expressions used within Stream's Routes
and Functions are written in Javascript. Javascript is
one of the most widely used Programming Languages
and while you don't need to be an expert in Javascript
knowing at least the basics of Javascript will help you
in your journey with using Cribl Stream.

10.2   Filter Language

Filters are Javascript Code that must result in a True or False value. Filters are used in both Routes and Functions to narrow the scope of data being selected to go down a Route or to be Processed by a specific Pipeline.

10.3   Expressions

Expressions are Javascript code that result in a value. Expressions can assign a value directly or can use code to perform calculations that result in a value.

Chapter 11

Cribl Search

Cribl Search is a powerful tool designed to provide efficient, scalable search capabilities across vast datasets. Its primary purpose is to enable users to perform rapid and flexible searches over large volumes of data without needing to send the data to expensive storage solutions. This is particularly valuable in environments where data is continuously ingested and needs to be analyzed quickly for insights.

11.1 Integration with Stream

While Cribl Stream focuses on data routing and transformation, Cribl Search complements it by offering advanced search capabilities. It allows users to query and analyze the data processed by Cribl Stream, making the data more accessible and actionable. This integration creates a seamless workflow from data ingestion to analysis.

Chapter 12

Projects

Cribl Stream Projects, also known as Stream Projects, offer a novel approach to data management within the Cribl Stream environment. They are designed to create isolated spaces for teams and users, enabling them to share and manage data efficiently and effectively. These projects provide project users with a streamlined visual UI, which is both user-friendly and adaptable to specific requirements. Administrators can finely tune user access to data and destinations, ensuring that access is relevant to the users' work.

12.1 Requirements

To enable the use of Projects within Cribl Stream, certain prerequisites must be met. The organization must possess either an Enterprise license and a distributed on-prem deployment or opt for a Cribl.Cloud Enterprise plan. This requirement ensures that the infrastructure and licensing are in place to support the advanced features and capabilities that Projects offer

12.2 Core Components

Projects in Cribl Stream are built upon several key components

- **Subscriptions**: These are used to filter a portion of a Worker Group's incoming data, making it available to project users along with various data processing options.

- **Data Projects**: This aspect involves the association of Subscriptions with specific Destinations. Both administrators and project users can utilize a drag-and-drop visual UI for connecting Subscriptions to chosen Destinations.

- **Roles and Policies**: Administrators are responsible for controlling user access to Subscriptions and Projects by assigning specific roles within Cribl Stream. Users assigned with the project_user role or the ProjectSourceSubscribe policy can view data through the Projects UI and have read access to data monitoring and notifications

Projects define what data a Project's users are allowed to interact with, where they can send that data, and who has access to the Project.

12.3 Getting Started with Projects

Engagement with Cribl Stream Projects varies based on the user's role.

Project Users: Upon logging into Cribl Stream and navigating to a Group, users will find their Subscriptions and Projects pre-configured in a visual UI. They can customize their Projects by connecting Subscriptions to Destinations and configuring Pipelines and Packs within their Worker Group.

Cribl Admins: Administrators access project configuration options by navigating to a Worker Group and selecting 'Manage > *<Your Group>* > Projects.' This action opens a submenu for Subscriptions and Data Projects, allowing for detailed configuration for project users.

12.4   Configuring Projects

Configuring Cribl Stream Projects involves defining the data accessible to users, specifying where the data can be sent, and determining who has access to the project. Each project associates specific Subscriptions with Destinations. For more precise access control, Projects can be shared with particular Members. The Project view in the UI allows administrators to manage connections among resources, add or commit projects, and manage Pipelines and Packs related to the project

To Configure a new Project you will need to go to a Worker Group. Then go to Manage, select Projects, and then open the default Data Projects Tab.

- From the Project view, click "Add Project" > "Add New Project"

- Assign the project a unique Project ID. All Project ID's are Case Sensitive. They can include _ and - characters. Spaces are not allowed.

- Select a single or multiple subscriptions.

- Select a single or multiple Destinations

- Add a Descriptions (This is not required, but I highly recommend it)

- Click the "Save" button.

- Don't forget to Commit and Deploy your Changes

12.5 Configuring Subscriptions

Subscriptions within Projects filter a subset of data from a Worker Group's incoming data stream and forward it to Destinations. Subscriptions can be associated with multiple Projects, each having independent data flow but sharing the same configuration. When configuring Subscriptions, differences from Routes should be noted, such as lacking a Route's Output field and not relaying backpressure upstream. It's important to consider the performance impact when adding Subscriptions, as each creates a copy of data for Cribl Stream to process.

To Configure a new Subscription and see existing Subscriptions you will need to go to a Worker Group. Then go to Manage, select Subscriptions.

Existing Configured Subscriptions will be present in this tab. Expand each section to see the Subscriptions Configuration. You can modify an existing Subscription by changing the values there.

- To add a new Subscriptions, while in the Subscription Tab, click "Add Subscription".

- Assign the project a unique Project ID. All Project ID's are Case Sensitive. They can include _ and - characters. Spaces are not allowed.

- Change the filter, replace the default "true" with a JavaScript expression that filters the events that you want to include in this Subscription.

- Change the Source's default passthru (unless that is the desired result)

- Add a Descriptions (This is not required, but I highly recommend it)

- Click the "Save" button.

- Don't forget to Commit and Deploy your Changes

12.6   Project Permissions

Stream Admins can modify Project Permissions.

Project-Level Permissions can be assigned based off the following permission sets.

Permission	Description
Maintainer	Admin-level Permission. Can edit the Project including and up to editing and deleting Project settings.
Editor	Can configure connections among the Project's Subscriptions, Packs, and Destinations. Cannot modify or delete resources. Can create, modify, and delete Pipelines within the Project.
Read Only	Can view Project and Subscription settings and connections, but not modify or delete them.
No Access	This is a Members default state for Projects that have not been shared with them. They will have no access to the Project.

Chapter 13

Datagens

Datagens give the user the capability to generate sample data to troubleshoot and develop your Routes, Pipelines, and Functions. Multiple datagens exist by default and new datagen templates can be created by users from existing Sample Data or Data Captures. Datagens are administered similarly to Sources.

13.1 Understanding Datagens

Datagens in Cribl Stream are used to generate sample data. Several datagen template files are included with Cribl Stream, and you can create more using sample files or live captures

13.2 Creating a Datagen Template from a Sample File

To create a new datagen template, go to the Preview Pane > Paste a Sample, and add a sample data entry. Next, from the Event Breaker drop-down, select an appropriate option to ensure proper event breaking and timestamp extraction.

13.3 Saving the Datagen Template

On the Create Datagen File screen, enter a file name and ensure the timestamp template format is correct. After verifying these details, click Save as Datagen File

13.4 Confirming Datagen Creation

To check if the datagen file has been successfully created, navigate to the Preview Pane > Datagens.

13.5 Using the Datagen File

To start using the newly created datagen file, return to Sources > Datagens and add it using the provided drop-down menu.

13.6 Modifying a Datagen

If you need to edit a datagen, select the Datagens tab in the Preview pane, hover over the file name you wish to modify, and click the edit button. This allows you to edit, clone, delete, or modify the datagen's metadata.

Chapter 14

Managing Stream License

In Cribl Stream, 'license usage' refers to the volume of data being transferred in and out of the product. Effective management of this aspect is crucial for optimizing resource utilization, maintaining optimal system performance, and ensuring adherence to licensing agreements.

14.1 Monitoring Overall License Usage

To monitor the overall license usage, open Cribl Stream Cloud and navigate to the Monitoring section. From there, select 'Overview'. In the top right corner of the dashboard, change the time frame from '15 min' to '1 day'. Now, you can view the chart that says 'Bytes In and Out'. The total number of Bytes in and Out combined represents your Cribl Stream license usage. This overview can also be seen on the Home Screen.

14.2 Monitoring License Usage by Source

To monitor the license usage of a specific source, navigate to 'Monitoring -> Data -> Source'. Again, change the time frame to '1 day'. Make sure the Source you want to view is selected. Then, look at the 'Total Bytes' column in the row containing your source. This will show you the license usage for that specific source.

14.3 Monitoring License Usage by Destination

To monitor the license usage of a specific destination, navigate to 'Monitoring -> Data -> Destination'. Change the time frame to '1 day' and ensure the Destination you want to view is selected. Look at the 'Total Bytes' column in the row containing your Destination. This will show you the license usage for that specific destination.

14.4 Monitoring License Usage by Route

To monitor the license usage of a specific route, navigate to 'Monitoring -> Data -> Routes'. Change the time frame to '1 day' and ensure the Route you want to view is selected. Look at the 'Total Bytes' column in the row containing your source. This will show you the license usage for that specific route.

14.5 Monitoring License Usage by Subscriptions

To monitor the license usage of a specific subscription, navigate to 'Monitoring -> Data -> Subscriptions'. Change the time frame to '1 day' and ensure the Subscription you want to view is selected. Look at the 'Total Bytes' column in the row containing your source. This will show you the license usage for that specific subscription.

14.6 Monitoring Top Talkers in Cribl Stream

To monitor the top talkers in Cribl Stream, navigate to 'Monitoring -> Reports -> Top Talkers'. Change the time frame to '1 day'. Look at the 'Total Bytes' column for each area you are interested in. This will show you the top talkers in Cribl Stream.

14.7 Monitoring by Worker & Worker Group

You can also view license usage by Worker and Worker Group by using the drop-down menus located next to the '1 Day' field in the upper right-hand corner. This allows you to get a more granular view of your license usage.

14.8 Viewing Data Flow Visualization

You can also view a visual representation of your data, navigate to 'Monitoring -> Flows'. Choose the Worker or worker group that you would like to see the visualization on. Change to Bytes. This can be useful to visually see what data is consuming license and how that data flows within the product. You can add and remove Sources, Routes, and Destinations from this chart.

Chapter 15

Stream UI Tools

15.1 Data Samples

Data Samples are small snippets of log data. You can upload samples of data you have received from another team as a file, or you can capture new data that has been pointed at Cribl Stream. You can then use this Sample Data to build your Routes and Pipelines to ensure they behave as you expect them to before you start sending live data to Production.

15.2   Data Sample Previews

Stream has functionality built in that allows you to view you Data Samples and see how Routes and Pipelines effect each event. You can see what the Sample Events look like when they come In, what the events look like when they go Out, and you can also see statistics on Event Size, Field Count, etc before and after processing by the Pipelines.

15.3   Live Capture

To capture data, you can click on the Capture button, assign a time period to perform the capture on and a maximum number of events to capture. Whichever condition it meets first will result in the capture being stopped and provide you with an option to save the capture. Captures default to aging out after 24 hours, but that can be changed to any number of hours and if set to a 0 will be kept indefinitely.

In the Capture Window to the left, you will see Symbols. These symbols are called Field Type Symbols and are meant to denote the type of data that each field contains.

- number = #
- ASCII/String = a
- Array = []

- Boolean (true/false) = b
- object = {}

Chapter 16

Special Considerations

This chapter is to highlight some very specific cases that are rare and unlikely to occur, but which might cause you some pain if they do. I will list these Scenarios out here to call them out.

Situation	Description
Downgrading from Enterprise Cloud	As of the writing of this book. If you have an Enterprise Cloud license and you downgrade from Enterprise Cloud to the free license your Enterprise Cloud account will be deleted in it's entirety. It is very important that you have all Packs, and other required data backed up Prior to downgrading.